JAN   2016

Insect World

Grasshoppers

by Mari Schuh

Bullfrog
Books

Ideas for Parents and Teachers

Bullfrog Books let children practice reading informational text at the earliest reading levels. Repetition, familiar words, and photo labels support early readers.

Before Reading

- Discuss the cover photo. What does it tell them?

- Look at the picture glossary together. Read and discuss the words.

Read the Book

- "Walk" through the book and look at the photos. Let the child ask questions. Point out the photo labels.

- Read the book to the child, or have him or her read independently.

After Reading

- Prompt the child to think more. Ask: Have you ever seen a grasshopper? Where was it? Did you hear it chirp?

The author dedicates this book to David and Alex Schuh.

Bullfrog Books are published by Jump!
5357 Penn Avenue South
Minneapolis, MN 55419
www.jumplibrary.com

Library of Congress Cataloging-in-Publication Data

Schuh, Mari C., 1975– author.
  Grasshoppers / by Mari Schuh.
    pages cm. — (Bullfrog books. Insect world)
  Includes index.
  Audience: Age 5.
  Audience: K to grade 3.
  ISBN 978-1-62031-162-2 (hardcover) —
  ISBN 978-1-62496-249-3 (ebook)
  1. Grasshoppers—Juvenile literature. I. Title.
II. Series: Schuh, Mari C., 1975– Insect world.
  QL508.A2S38 2015
  595.7'26—dc23
                                     2014032114

Series Editor: Rebecca Glaser
Series Designer: Ellen Huber
Book Designer: Anna Peterson
Photo Researcher: Casie Cook

Photo Credits: All photos by Shutterstock except: Corbis, 3, 8–9, 14–15, 16–17, 23tl, 23bl, 23br; Dwight Kuhn/Kuhn Photo, 12–13, 23tr; Nature Picture Library, 6–7; Thinkstock, 24.

Printed in the United States of America at Corporate Graphics, in North Mankato, Minnesota.

Table of Contents

Chirping Bugs

Chirp! Chirp!

A grasshopper sings
in the tall grass.

He rubs his back legs
on his wings.

His song is loud.

He sings all day.

Why?

He sings to find a female.

female

Oh, no!
A hungry bird!

The grasshopper hides.
He blends in with the grass.

spit

The grasshopper spits.
Yuck!
It scares the bird.

The grasshopper leaps.
Its long legs stretch out.
It jumps high and far.

Then the grasshopper
flies away.

Look at it go!

See the antennas?
They smell for food.

antenna

The grasshopper
finds leaves to eat.

Now he rests.

He will sing again soon.

Chirp! Chirp!

Parts of a Grasshopper

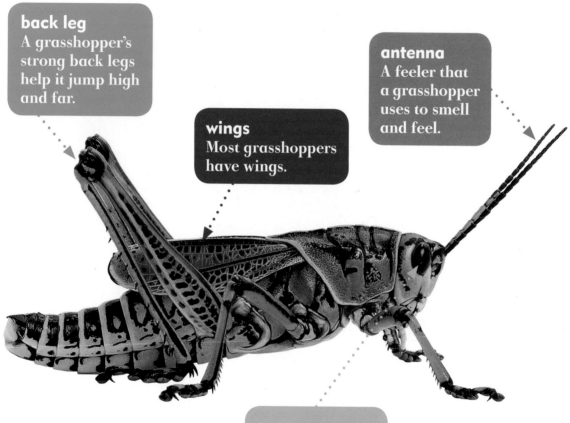

back leg
A grasshopper's strong back legs help it jump high and far.

wings
Most grasshoppers have wings.

antenna
A feeler that a grasshopper uses to smell and feel.

eyes
Grasshoppers have two big eyes that let them see forward, to the side, and behind.

Picture Glossary

female
An insect or animal that can give birth to young animals or lay eggs.

spit
To force liquid out of the mouth.

leap
To jump.

stretch
To spread out a body part.

Index

To Learn More

Learning more is as easy as 1, 2, 3.

1) Go to www.factsurfer.com

2) Enter "grasshoppers" into the search box.

3) Click the "Surf" button to see a list of websites.

With factsurfer.com, finding more information is just a click away.